CW00468579

Air Fryer Green Meals

40+ Quick Plant-Based Recipes For The Air Fryer That Will Make Your Life Easier

Christopher Ramsay

TABLE OF CONTENTS

Air Fryer Green Meals Recipes

Baby Potatoes Mix

Preparation time: 10 minutes Cooking time: 20 minutes Servings: 4

INGREDIENTS

- 1 pound baby potatoes, peeled and halved 1 cup green beans, trimmed and halved
- cup corn
- tablespoons avocado oil Juice of 1 lime
- Salt and black pepper to the taste 3 garlic cloves, minced

- ½ teaspoon rosemary, dried 1 teaspoon turmeric powder 1 tablespoon dill, chopped

DIRECTIONS

1. In the air fryer's pan, mix the potatoes with the green beans and the other ingredients, toss and cook at 400 degrees F for 20 minutes.

2. Divide between plates and serve. **NUTRITION:** Calories 171, Fat 5, Fiber 6, Carbs 15, Protein 8

Cabbage Salad

Preparation time: 10 minutes Cooking time: 15 minutes Servings: 4

INGREDIENTS

- 1 pound red cabbage, shredded 1 red onion, sliced
- 1 cup carrots, peeled and shredded Juice of 1 lime
- tablespoon olive oil
- ¼ teaspoon sweet paprika
- Salt and black pepper to the taste 1 tablespoon dill, chopped

DIRECTIONS

1. In a pan that fits your air fryer, mix the cabbage with the onion and the other ingredients , toss, introduce the pan in the fryer and cook at 400 degrees F for 15 minutes.

2. Divide into bowls and serve.

NUTRITION: Calories 154, Fat 4, Fiber 4, Carbs 12, Protein 5

Cabbage and Pomegranate Mix

Preparation time: 10 minutes Cooking time: 12 minutes Servings: 4

INGREDIENTS

- 1 pound green cabbage, shredded
- ¼ cup butter, melted
- 1 cup pomegranate seeds
- 1 tablespoon chives, chopped
- A pinch of salt and black pepper 1 tablespoon sweet paprika
- 1 tablespoon dill, chopped

DIRECTIONS

1. In a pan that fits your air fryer, mix the cabbage with the butter and the other ingredients, toss, introduce the pan in the fryer and cook at 380 degrees F for 12 minutes.

2. Divide everything into bowls and serve. **NUTRITION**: Calories 181, Fat 4, Fiber 6, Carbs 15, Protein 5

Kale Salad

Preparation time: 4 minutes Cooking time: 15 minutes
Servings: 4

INGREDIENTS

- 1 pound baby kale 1 cup corn
- 1 cup cherry tomatoes, halved 1 tablespoon olive oil
- Juice of 1 lime
- Salt and black pepper to the taste
- ½ cup spring onions, chopped

DIRECTIONS

1. In a pan that fits your air fryer, mix the kale with the corn and the other ingredients, toss, introduce the pan in the fryer and cook at 350 degrees F for 15 minutes.

2. Divide the salad into bowls and serve.

NUTRITION: Calories 151, Fat 4, Fiber 5, Carbs 15, Protein 6

Air Fried Grilled Asparagus

Servings: 1

Cooking Time: 15 minutes

INGREDIENTS

- ½ bunch asparagus spears, trimmed Salt and pepper to taste
- 1 tablespoon olive oil

DIRECTIONS

1. Preheat the air fryer at 375oF.
2. Place the grill pan accessory in the air fryer. Season the asparagus with salt and pepper.
3. Drizzle with oil.

4. Place on the grill pan and cook for 15 minutes.

5. Give the air fryer a good shake to cook evenly.

NUTRITION: Calories: 138; Carbs: 4.3g; Protein: 0.9g; Fat: 13.5g

Grilled Hasselback Potatoes

Servings: 1

Cooking Time: 25 minutes

INGREDIENTS

- 1 large potato
- 1 tablespoon butter
- ½ tablespoon oil
- Salt and pepper to taste

DIRECTIONS

1. Preheat the air fryer at 3750F.
2. Place the grill pan accessory in the air fryer.

3. Place the potato on a cutting board. Place chopsticks on each side of the potato and slice until where the cut marks are.

4. Brush potato with butter and oil. Season with salt and pepper to taste.

5. Place on the grill pan and cook for 20 to 25 minutes

NUTRITION: Calories: 464; Carbs: 68.7g; Protein: 8.7g; Fat: 18.6g

Air Fryer Roasted Vegetables

Servings: 4

Cooking Time: 15 minutes

INGREDIENTS

- 1 teaspoon olive oil
- 1 bunch asparagus spears, trimmed
- 1 yellow squash, seeded and cut in circles 1 zucchini, seeded and cut in circles
- 1 cup button mushrooms, quartered
- Salt and pepper to taste
- 1 teaspoon basil powder 1 teaspoon thyme

DIRECTIONS

1. Preheat the air fryer at 375OF.

2. Place the grill pan accessory in the air fryer.

3. Mix all vegetables in a bowl and toss to coat everything with the seasoning.

4. Place on the grill pan and cook for 15 minutes.

5. Make sure to stir the vegetables halfway through the cooking time.

NUTRITION: Calories: 38; Carbs: 5.8g; Protein: 1.8g; Fat: 1.5g

Air Fried Roasted Summer Squash

Servings: 2

Preparation Time: 5 minutes Cooking Time: 15 minutes

INGREDIENTS

• 1-pound zucchini, sliced into rounds or circles 2 tablespoons extra virgin olive oil

• 1 teaspoon salt

• ½ teaspoon black pepper 1 teaspoon garlic powder

DIRECTIONS

1. Preheat the air fryer at 3750F.

2. Place the grill pan accessory in the air fryer.

3. In a mixing bowl, toss all ingredients until well-combined.

4. Place on the grill pan and cook for 15 minutes.

5. Stir the vegetables halfway through the cooking time.

NUTRITION: Calories:109; Carbs: 8.6g; Protein: 6.9g; Fat: 6.5g

Indian Grilled Vegetables

Servings: 6

Cooking Time: 20 minutes

INGREDIENTS

- ½ cup yogurt
- cloves of garlic, minced
- 2-inch fresh ginger, minced
- 3 tablespoons Tandoori spice blend
- 2 tablespoons canola oil

- 2 small onions, cut into wedges
- 1 small zucchini, cut into thick slices

- 1 carrot, peeled and shaved to 1/8-inch thick 1 yellow sweet pepper, seeded and chopped
- ½ head cauliflower, cut into florets 1 handful sugar snap peas
- 1 cup young ears of corn

DIRECTIONS

1   Preheat the air fryer at 350oF.

2   Place the grill pan accessory in the air fryer.

3   In a Ziploc bag, put all ingredients and give a shake to season all vegetables.

4   Dump all ingredients on the grill pan and cook for 20 minutes.

5   Make sure to give the vegetables a shake halfway through the cooking time.

NUTRITION: Calories:126; Carbs: 17.9g; Protein: 2.9g; Fat: 6.1g

Grilled Sweet Potato Wedges with Dipping Sauce

Servings: 3

Cooking Time: 20 minutes

INGREDIENTS

- 3 medium sweet potatoes, peeled and sliced 2 tablespoons olive oil
- Salt and pepper to taste
- ½ cup sour cream
- ½ cup mayonnaise
- 2 tablespoons fresh chives, chopped 3 tablespoons Asiago cheese, grated 2 tablespoons parmesan cheese

DIRECTIONS

1   Preheat the air fryer at 3500F.

2   Place the grill pan accessory in the air fryer.

3   Brush the potatoes with olive oil and drizzle with salt and pepper to taste.

4   Place on the grill pan and cook for 20 minutes.

5   Meanwhile, mix the sour cream, mayonnaise, fresh chives, Asiago cheese, and parmesan cheese in a bowl.

6 Season with salt and pepper to taste.

7 Serve the potatoes with the sauce.

NUTRITION: Calories: 625; Carbs: 50.5g; Protein: 12.7g; Fat: 42.3g

Grilled Green Beans with Shallots

Servings: 6

Cooking Time: 25 minutes

INGREDIENTS

- 1-pound fresh green beans, trimmed 2 large shallots, sliced
- 1 tablespoon vegetable oil 1 teaspoon soy sauce
- 2 tablespoons fresh basil, chopped
- 1 tablespoon fresh mint, chopped
- 1 tablespoon sesame seeds, toasted 2 tablespoons pine nuts

DIRECTIONS

1 Preheat the air fryer at 3500F.

2 Place the grill pan accessory in the air fryer. In a mixing bowl, combine the green beans,

3 shallots, vegetable oil, and soy sauce.

4   Dump in the air fryer and cook for 25 minutes.

5   Once cooked, garnish with basil, mints, sesame seeds, and pine nuts.

NUTRITION: Calories:307; Carbs: 11.2g; Protein: 23.7g; Fat: 19.7g

Grille Tomatoes with Garden Herb Salad

Servings: 4

Cooking Time: 20 minutes

INGREDIENTS

- 3 large green tomatoes 1 clove of garlic, minced 5 tablespoons olive oil Salt and pepper to taste
- ¾ cup fresh parsley, chopped
- ¾ cup cilantro leaves, chopped
- ½ cup chopped chives 4 leaves iceberg lettuce
- ¼ cup hazelnuts, toasted and chopped
- ¼ cup pistachios, toasted and chopped
- ¼ cup golden raisins
- 2 tablespoons white balsamic vinegar

DIRECTIONS

1 Preheat the air fryer at 350oF.
2 Place the grill pan accessory in the air fryer.
3 In a mixing bowl, season the tomatoes with garlic, oil, salt and pepper to taste.

4 Place on the grill pan and grill for 20 minutes.

5 Once the tomatoes are done, toss in a salad bowl together with the rest of the ingredients.

NUTRITION: Calories: 287; Carbs: 12.2g; Protein: 4.8g; Fat: 25.9g

Grilled Potato Packets

Servings: 3

Cooking Time: 40 minutes

INGREDIENTS

- 2 large russet potatoes, peeled and sliced 2 medium red sweet potatoes, sliced
- 1 onion, sliced
- 2 tablespoons olive oil
- 1 ½ teaspoons seasoning blend Salt and pepper to taste

DIRECTIONS

1   Preheat the air fryer at 3500F.

2   Place the grill pan accessory in the air fryer.

3   Take a large piece of foil and place all ingredients in the middle.

4   Give a good stir. Fold the foil and crimp the edges.

5   Place the foil on the grill pan. Cook for 40 minutes.

NUTRITION: Calories: 362; Carbs: 68.4g; Protein: 6.3g; Fat: 9.4g

Grilled Sweet Onions

Servings: 2

Cooking Time: 30 minutes

INGREDIENTS

- 2 large sweet onions, sliced
- ½ cup ranch salad dressing
- 2 tablespoons Worcestershire sauce 1 teaspoon salad seasoning

DIRECTIONS

1   Preheat the air fryer at 3500F.

2   Place the grill pan accessory in the air fryer.

3   Place all ingredients in a mixing bowl and give a good stir.

4   Allow the onions to marinate in the fridge for at least 30 minutes.

5   Dump on the grill pan and cook for 30 minutes.

NUTRITION: Calories:342; Carbs: 20.8g; Protein: 2.5g; Fat: 4g

Roasted Dill Potato Medley

Servings: 3

Cooking Time: 30 minutes

INGREDIENTS

- 3 Yukon gold potatoes, scrubbed and cut into 1-inch pieces
- 1 ½ cups peeled baby carrots, peeled and sliced
- 1 cup frozen pearl onions, peeled and sliced 4 tablespoons olive oil

- 2 tablespoons snipped fresh dill, chopped 1 teaspoon salt

- ½ teaspoon black pepper 1 lemon, juiced

DIRECTIONS

1 Preheat the air fryer at 3500F.

2 Place the grill pan accessory in the air fryer.

3 Season the vegetables with the rest of the ingredients.

4 Place on the grill pan and cook for 30 minutes.

5 Be sure to shake the vegetables every 5 minutes to cook evenly.

NUTRITION: Calories: 480; Carbs: 72.4g; Protein: 8.7g; Fat: 19.1g

Grilled Squash

Servings: 3

Cooking Time: 20 minutes

INGREDIENTS

- 3 zucchinis, cut into quarters
- 1 onion, sliced
- ounces fresh mushrooms, stems removed and sliced
- 1 tablespoon oil
- Salt and pepper to taste
- ½ cup Italian salad dressing

DIRECTIONS

- Preheat the air fryer at 3500F.
- Place the grill pan accessory in the air fryer.
- Season the zucchini, onion, and mushrooms with oil, salt, and pepper.
- Place on the grill pan and cook for 20 minutes.
- Serve with Italian salad dressing.

NUTRITION: Calories: 367; Carbs: 63.7g; Protein:8.1 g; Fat: 13.6g

Air Fryer Grilled Fennel

Servings: 2

Cooking Time: 20 minutes

INGREDIENTS

- 2 medium fennel bulbs, peeled and sliced 2 tablespoons olive oil
- 3 tablespoons lemon juice Salt and pepper to taste
- cloves of garlic, minced

DIRECTIONS

1   Preheat the air fryer at 3500F.
2   Place the grill pan accessory in the air fryer.

3   Place all ingredients in a mixing bowl until the fennel slices are well- seasoned.

4   Dump on the grill pan and cook for 20 minutes.

NUTRITION: Calories:215; Carbs: 22.7g; Protein: 3.8g; Fat: 14.1g

Grilled Corn Kabobs

Servings: 2

Cooking Time: 25 minutes

INGREDIENTS

- 2 ears of corn
- 2 medium green peppers, cut into large chunks
- 1-pound apricots, halved Salt and pepper to taste
- 2 teaspoons prepared mustard

DIRECTIONS

1 Preheat the air fryer at 350oF.
2 Place the grill pan accessory in the air fryer.

3 On the double layer rack with the

skewer accessories, skewer the corn, green peppers, and

apricots.

4 Season with salt and pepper to taste.

5 Place skewered corn on the double layer rack and

cook for 25 minutes.

6 Once cooked, brush with prepared mustard.

NUTRITION: Calories: 341; Carbs: 82.5g; Protein:

7.43g; Fat: 2.2g

Grill Smoked Mushrooms

Servings: 4

Cooking Time: 30 minutes

INGREDIENTS

- cups sliced mushrooms
- ¼ cup butter
- 1 teaspoon liquid smoke
- 1 teaspoon poultry seasoning Salt and pepper to taste

DIRECTIONS

1 Preheat the air fryer at 3500F.

2 Place the grill pan accessory in the air fryer.

3 Place all ingredients in a large piece of aluminum foil and mix until well- combined.

4 Close the foil and crimp the edges.

5 Place on the grill pan and cook for 30 minutes.

NUTRITION: Calories: 109; Carbs:1.5 g; Protein: 0.5g; Fat: 11.6g

Mushroom Dip

Preparation time: 5 minutes Cooking time: 20 minutes

Servings: 4

INGREDIENTS

- 2 tablespoons balsamic vinegar 2 pounds mushrooms, chopped 1 cup heavy cream
- 2 tablespoons olive oil
- ½ teaspoon basil, dried
- ½ teaspoon thyme, dried
- A pinch of salt and black pepper

DIRECTIONS

1. In the air fryer's pan, mix the mushrooms with the vinegar and the other ingredients, whisk, put the pan in the machine and cook at 380 degrees F for 20 minutes.

2. Divide into bowls and serve as a party dip.

NUTRITION: Calories 147, Fat 8, Fiber 2,

Carbs 3,

Protein 3

Shrimp and Radish Mix

Preparation time: 5 minutes Cooking time: 20 minutes
Servings: 4

INGREDIENTS

- 1 pound shrimp, peeled, deveined and minced
- 1 cup radishes, halved
- ½ cup spring onions, chopped 1 tablespoon olive oil
- 1 tablespoon lemon juice
- 1 tablespoon parsley, chopped Salt and black pepper
to the taste

DIRECTIONS

1. In the air fryer's pan, mix the shrimp with the radishes and the other ingredients, put the pan in the machine and cook at 360 degrees F for 14 minutes.

2. Divide into bowls and serve as an appetizer.

NUTRITION: Calories 271, Fat 15, Fiber 3, Carbs 4, Protein 14

Tuna and Shrimp Mix

Preparation time: 5 minutes Cooking time: 10 minutes

Servings: 2

INGREDIENTS

- 1 pound tuna, skinless, boneless and cubed
- ½ pound shrimp, peeled and deveined 1 cup cherry tomatoes, halved
- 1 cup baby spinach
- 1 chili pepper, minced 2 tablespoon olive oil
- 1 tablespoon lemon juice
- A pinch of salt and black pepper

DIRECTIONS

1. In a pan that fits your air fryer, mix all the ingredients, toss, introduce in the fryer and cook at 360 degrees F for 10 minutes.

2. Divide into bowls and serve as an

appetizer.

NUTRITION: Calories 231, Fat 18, Fiber 3, Carbs 4, Protein 18

Avocado and Green Beans Bowls

Preparation time: 5 minutes Cooking time: 12 minutes

Servings: 4

INGREDIENTS

- 2 avocados, peeled, pitted and cut into wedges
- ½ pound green beans, trimmed and halved 1 cup kalamata olives, pitted and halved
- 1 cup cherry tomatoes, halved 1 tablespoon olive oil
- A pinch of salt and black pepper

DIRECTIONS

1. In the air fryer's pan, mix the avocados with the green beans and the other ingredients, toss, put the pan in the

2. machine and cook at 370 degrees F for 12 minutes.

3. Divide into bowls and serve as an appetizer.

NUTRITION: Calories 200, Fat 12, Fiber 3, Carbs 5, Protein 16

Bacon Dip

Preparation time: 5 minutes Cooking time: 20 minutes
Servings: 8

INGREDIENTS

- 2 tablespoons butter, melted 1 cup cream cheese, soft
- 1 cup bacon, chopped
- ½ teaspoon sweet paprika
- 3 cups spring onions, chopped A pinch of salt and
black pepper 1 tablespoon chives, chopped

DIRECTIONS

1. In the air fryer's pan, mix the melted butter with the bacon and the other ingredients, introduce the pan in the machine and cook at and 380 degrees F for 20 minutes.

2. Divide into bowls and serve as a party dip.

NUTRITION: Calories 220, Fat 12, Fiber 2, Carbs 4, Protein 15

Crab Dip

Preparation time: 5 minutes Cooking time: 20 minutes

Servings: 4

INGREDIENTS

- 1 cup cream cheese, soft 1 cup crab meat
- 1 tablespoon lemon juice
- 1 bunch green onions, minced
- ½ teaspoon turmeric powder
- A pinch of salt and black pepper 1 tablespoon

chives, chopped

DIRECTIONS

- In the air fryer's pan, mix the cream cheese with the crab meat and the other ingredients, introduce the pan in the machine and cook at 380 degrees F for 20 minutes.
- Divide the mix into bowls and serve as a party dip.

NUTRITION: Calories 240, Fat 8, Fiber 2, Carbs 4,Protein 14

Rice spaghetti with vegetables

Preparation time: 10 – 20 minutes

Cooking time: 15 – 30 minutes

Servings: 4

INGREDIENTS

- 100 g of celery
- 150 g of carrots
- 150g kale
- 2 scallions
- 2 tbsp soy sauce
- 100 g of bean sprouts
- 200 g of rice spaghetti

DIRECTIONS

1. Spray the basket of the air fryer. Cut all the vegetables in julienne and put the celery, chives, and carrots in the basket.

2. Set the air fryer to 150oC. Cook for 10 minutes.

3. Add the sprouts and soy sauce and cook for another 10 minutes.

4. Meanwhile, cook the rice spaghetti in salted water and boil and serve with the previously prepared sauce.

NUTRITION: Calories 235.0 Fat 10.9 G Carbohydrate 34.7 G Sugars 6.4 G Protein13.9 G Cholesterol 0.5 Mg

Strapatsada

Preparation time: 10-20 minutes Cooking time: 15-30 minutes Servings: 4

INGREDIENTS

- ½ onion
- 1 red pepper
- 100g mushrooms
- 300 g of tomatoes
- 6 eggs
- Fine salt to taste
- Black pepper to taste

DIRECTIONS

1. Cut the mushrooms (washed) and onions in julienne.

2. Distribute everything in the tank with the oil.

3. Set the temperature to 1800C and Cook for 12 minutes.

4. Add the tomatoes (skinless) cut into pieces, salt, and cook for another 8 minutes.

5. Remove the trowel (take care that it is hot!) And distribute the vegetables at the basket.

6. In a bowl, beat the eggs with salt and pepper and pour all over the vegetables. Cook another 7 to 8 minutes.

NUTRITION: Calories 380 Carbohydrates Fat 30g Sugars 6g Protein 19g Cholesterol 370g

. Chicory Strudel

Preparation time: 10-20 minutes Cooking time: 30-45 minutes Servings: 6

INGREDIENTS

- 1 puff pastry
- Red chicory
- 100 g of stravecchio cheese
- 100 g of cow mozzarella
- 3 slices of Italian stuffed piglet

DIRECTIONS

1. Unroll the puff pastry, cover with a layer of cheese shavings, add the pieces of raw chicory and diced mozzarella.

2. Cover the whole with slices of stuffed piglet and close the puff pastry to form a stake.

3. Place the lining on the baking paper inside the basket.

4. Set the temperature to 1600C and cook for 35 minutes.

5. Very good with cheese sauce.

NUTRITION: Calories 210 Carbohydrates 30g Fat 5g Sugars 10g Protein 9g Cholesterol 0mg

Toast with Eggplant Caviar

Preparation time: 10-20 minutes Cooking time: 15-30 minutes

Servings: 8

INGREDIENTS

- Eggplants 450g
- 1 tbsp concentrated tomatoes
- 100 g almonds
- 1 shallot
- 25 g of Parmesan
- 15 basil leaves
- Bread slices

DIRECTIONS

1. Cut the shallot finely and pour it into the basket previously greased with the spray.

2. Brown for 2 minutes at 160oC.

3. Add chopped eggplants, tomato puree diluted in 100 ml of water, salt and cook for 23 minutes.

4. Chill the eggplants after cooking. Place the almonds in the basket and roast them for 4 to 5 minutes.

5. Mix eggplant with almonds, parmesan, and basil separately until a homogeneous compound is obtained.

6. Remove the preparation paddle from the tank (be careful, it will be hot), place the slices of bread inside and roast them for 4 to 5 minutes or until golden brown.

7. Fill each crust with the previously prepared sauce.

NUTRITION: Calories 91.8 Fat 6.1 G Carbohydrate 9.2 G Sugars0.0 G Protein 1.5 G Cholesterol 1.3 Mg

Provencal Tomatoes

Preparation time: 10 – 20 minutes

Cooking time: 15 – 30 minutes

Servings: 4

INGREDIENTS

- 4 tomatoes
- 80 g of breadcrumbs
- 1 clove garlic
- 2 marjoram branches
- 1 rosemary branch
- Parsley chopped to taste
- Salt to taste
- Butter to taste

DIRECTIONS

1. Remove the top of the tomatoes and drain them. Separately, place all other ingredients (except butter) in a bowl and mix them; The mixture must be quite sandy.

2. Fill the tomatoes and then place them in

the basket by adding the butter.

3. Set the temperature to 1600C and cook for 20 minutes depending on the size of the tomatoes.

4. It can be served both cold and hot.

NUTRITION: Calories 69 Carbohydrates 8g Fat 2g Sugars 2g Protein 3g Cholesterol 7g

Potato Omelet

Preparation time: 10 – 20 minutes

Cooking time: 15 – 30 minutes

Servings: 6

INGREDIENTS

- 600 g of potatoes
- ½ onion
- 6 eggs
- Salt, pepper to taste

DIRECTIONS

1. Peel the potatoes and cut them into squares of approximately 1 cm; Peel the onion and cut it into slices that are not very thin.

2. Pour the onion, oil and potatoes in the basket Cook for 25 minutes at 160oC.

3. Distribute potatoes and onion well in the bottom of the basket. Then pour the previously made egg, salt, and pepper mixture. Continue cooking for another 5 minutes.

NUTRITION: Calories 193 Carbohydrates 27g Fat 5g Sugars 1g Protein 10g Cholesterol 185 Mg

Vol Au Vent with Mushrooms

Preparation time: 10 - 20 minutes

Cooking time: 15 – 30 minutes

Servings: 6

INGREDIENTS

- 1 roll of puff pastry
- Whole milk to taste
- 100 g of air sautéed mushrooms and parsley
- Brie to taste

DIRECTIONS

1. Unroll the puff pastry, prick the bottom with a fork and cut 18 discs about 7 cm in diameter. Place 6 discs in the bowl covered with baking paper.

2. Make a hole of approximately 3 cm in

the other 12 discs and place them two at a

3. time in the large discs. Brush with milk so that they adhere well to each other.

4. Set the temperature to 1600C

5. Cook for 15 to 17 minutes. Rotate the baking paper after 10 minutes for best results.

6. Fill the vol au vent with a preparation of mushrooms sautéed in air and parsley and cover with a piece of cheese.

7. Serve still hot

NUTRITION: Calories 94 Fat 6.4g Carbohydrates 6.7g Protein 1.7g

Spanish Potatoes

Preparation time: 10 minutes

Cooking time: 57 minutes Servings: 2

INGREDIENTS

- 400 g potato
- Water
- 1 tbsp olive oil
- Salt

DIRECTIONS

1. Peel and cut the potato in julienne about

2. 0.5 CM thick.

3. Prepare a bowl with very cold water, if necessary, add ice. Place the cut potatoes for at least 30 minutes to make them starch.

4. Dry each potato with an absorbent napkin and place in another dry bowl.

5. When they are all dry, sprinkle with oil or brush with olive oil and season with salt and whatever you like (sweet paprika, oregano, etc.).

6. In this case place in a fryer without oil at temperature 1600C for 17 minutes.

7. Set the fryer at 1800C another 10 minutes and that's it.

NUTRITION: Calories   77   Fat   0.09g
Carbohydrate17.47g   Sugars   0.78g   Protein2.02g
Cholesterol 0mg

Green Salad with Roasted Pepper

Preparation time: 15 minutes

Cooking time: 10 minutes Servings: 4

INGREDIENTS

- 1 red pepper
- 1 tbsp lemon juice

- 3 tbsp yogurt
- 2 tbsp olive oil
- Freshly ground black pepper
- 1 romaine lettuce in wide strips
- 50 g arugula leaves

DIRECTIONS

1. Preheat the air fryer to 200°C.

2. Place the pepper in the basket and place it in the air fryer. Set the timer to 10 minutes and roast the pepper until the skin is slightly burned.

3. Place the pepper in a bowl and cover it with a lid or with transparent film. Let stand 10 to 15 minutes.

4. Next, cut the pepper into four parts and remove the seeds and skin. Cut the pepper into strips.

5. Mix a dressing in a bowl with 2 tablespoons of the pepper juice, lemon juice, yogurt, and olive oil. Add pepper and salt to taste.

6. Pour the lettuce and arugula leaves into the dressing and garnish the salad with the pepper strips.

NUTRITION: Calories 77.9 Fat 0.4 G Carbohydrate 19.3 G Sugars4.6 G Protein2.7 G Cholesterol 0.0 Mg

Garlic Mushrooms

Preparation time: 10 minutes

Cooking time: 10 minutes Servings: 2

INGREDIENTS

- 1 slice of white bread
- 1 crushed garlic clove
- 1 tbsp chopped parsley
- Freshly ground black pepper

- 1 tbsp olive oil
- 12 mushrooms

DIRECTIONS

1. Preheat the air fryer to 200°C.

2. Grate the slice of bread until it is thin in the kitchen robot and mix it with the garlic, parsley, and season to taste. Finally, pour the olive oil.

3. Remove the mushroom stems and fill the caps with the breadcrumbs.

4. Place the mushrooms in the basket and place it in the air fryer. Set the timer to 10

minutes. Bake until golden brown and crispy.

5. Serve them on a tray.

NUTRITION: Calories 139 Fat 11.6g Carbohydrates 6.1g Sugars 3.5gprotein 4.7g Cholesterol 30.4mg

Roasted Potatoes with Paprika and Greek Yogurt

Preparation time: 10 minutes

Cooking time: 20 minutes Servings: 4

INGREDIENTS

- 800 g of white potatoes
- 2 tbsp olive oil
- 1 tbsp spicy paprika
- Freshly ground black pepper
- 150 ml Greek yogurt

DIRECTIONS

1. Preheat the air fryer to 1800C. Peel the potatoes and cut them into cubes of 3 cm. Dip the cubes in water for at least 30 minutes. Dry them well with paper towels.

2. In a medium-sized bowl, mix 1 tablespoon of olive oil with the paprika and add pepper to taste. Coat the potato dice with the spiced oil.

3. Place the potato dice in the fryer basket and place it in the air fryer. Set the timer to 20 minutes and fry the dice until golden brown and ready to take. Spin them

occasionally.

4. In a small bowl, mix the Greek yogurt with the remaining tablespoon of olive oil and add salt and pepper to taste. Spread the paprika over the mixture. Serve the yogurt as a sauce with the potatoes.

5. Serve the potato dice on a tray and salt them. They will be delicious with ribs or kebabs.

NUTRITION: Calories 225.1 Fat 13.8 G Carbohydrate 24.2 G Sugars 9.7 G Protein2.5 G Cholesterol 0.0 Mg

Mini peppers with Goat Cheese

Preparation time: 10 minutes

Cooking time: 8 minutes Servings: 4

INGREDIENTS

- 8 mini peppers
- ½ tbsp olive oil
- ½ tbsp dried Italian herbs
- 1 tsp freshly ground black pepper
- 100 g soft goat cheese in eight portions

DIRECTIONS

1. Preheat the air fryer to 200°C.

2. Cut the top of the mini peppers and remove the seeds and the membrane.

3. Mix the olive oil in a deep dish with the Italian herbs and pepper. Pour the portions of goat cheese in the oil.

4. Press a serving of goat cheese against each mini pepper and place the mini peppers in the basket next to each other. Insert the basket in the air fryer and set the timer to 8 minutes. Bake the mini peppers until the cheese is melted.

5. Serve mini peppers in small dishes such as snacks or snacks.

NUTRITION: Calories 17 Fat 1g Carbohydrates 1g Sugar 1g Protein 0g Cholesterol 60mg

Lemony Green Beans

Cooking Time: 12 minutes Servings: 4

INGREDIENTS

- 1 lb. green beans washed and destemmed
- Sea salt and black pepper to taste
- 1 lemon
- ¼ teaspoon extra virgin olive oil

DIRECTIONS

1. Preheat your air fryer to 400° Fahrenheit. Place the green beans in the air fryer basket.

Squeeze lemon over beans and season with salt and pepper. Cover ingredients with oil and toss well. Cook green beans for 12- minutes and serve!

NUTRITION: Calories: 263, Total Fat: 9.2g, Carbs: 8.6g, Protein: 8.7g

Roasted Orange Cauliflower

Cooking Time: 20 minutes Servings: 2

INGREDIENTS

- 1 head cauliflower
- ½ lemon, juiced
- ½ tablespoon olive oil
- 1 teaspoon curry powder
- Sea salt and black pepper to taste

DIRECTIONS

Prepare your cauliflower by washing and removing the leaves and core. Slice it into florets of comparable size. Grease your air fryer with oil and preheat it for 2-minutes at 390°Fahrenheit. Combine fresh lemon juice and curry powder, add the cauliflower florets and stir. Use salt and pepper as seasoning and stir again. Cook for 20- minutes and serve warm.

Eggplant Parmesan Panini

Cooking Time: 25 minutes Servings: 2

INGREDIENTS

- 1 medium eggplant, cut into ½ inch slices
- ½ cup mayonnaise
- 2 tablespoons milk
- Black pepper to taste
- ½ teaspoon garlic powder
- ½ teaspoon onion powder
- 1 tablespoon dried parsley
- ½ teaspoon Italian seasoning
- ½ cup breadcrumbs
- Sea salt to taste
- Fresh basil, chopped for garnishing
- ¾ cup tomato sauce
- 2 tablespoons parmesan, grated cheese
- 2 cups grated mozzarella cheese
- 2 tablespoons olive oil
- 4 slices artisan Italian bread
- Cooking spray

DIRECTIONS

1.   Cover both sides of eggplant with salt. Place them between sheets of paper towels. Set aside for 30-minutes to get rid of excess moisture. In a mixing bowl, combine Italian seasoning, breadcrumbs, parsley, onion powder, garlic powder and season with salt and pepper. In another small bowl, whisk mayonnaise and milk until smooth.

2.   Preheat your air fryer to 400°Fahrenheit. Remove the excess salt from eggplant slices. Cover both sides of eggplant with mayonnaise mixture. Press the eggplant slices into the breadcrumb mixture. Use

cooking spray on both sides of eggplant slices. Air fry slices in batches for 15- minutes, turning over when halfway done. Each bread slice must be greased with olive oil. On a cutting board, place two slices of bread with oiled sides down. Layer mozzarella cheese and grated parmesan cheese. Place eggplant on cheese. Cover with tomato sauce and add remaining mozzarella and parmesan cheeses. Garnish with chopped fresh basil. Put the second slice of bread oiled side up on top.

Take preheated Panini press and place sandwiches on it. Close the lid and cook for 10-minutes. Slice panini into halves and serve.

NUTRITION: Calories: 267, Total Fat: 11.3g, Carbs: 8.7g, Protein: 8.5g